SIGNATURE PAGE

DEDICATION

I would like to dedicate this book to my younger self. We had great fun learning life the hard way. I will miss you, but like time, we must move forward.

A STROKE OF RECOVERY

MEETRI'AANGELO

INTRODUCTION

My name is Meetri'a Angelo. You are about to read a story that I wrote throughout 2023. When I was thirty-six years old, a major stroke hit me and overnight changed my life forever. Friday, January 13, 2023, was a day that stopped me in my tracks. I never imagined the impact of a stroke on me at that age. I never imagined the impact of a stroke at all. We don't really talk about these things. Strokes always happened to someone else. This is a story of my personal experiences during this devastating time. I am not a therapist or a counselor in the mental health profession, but I feel I am a person with a high EQ, and I have a relatable story of recovery and perseverance.

When the stroke hit me, I was beyond terrified! I wanted to know how others survived it or even if anyone ever had survived it at all. I went in search of stories similar to mine. I couldn't find any. There were stories of people who had had strokes and recovered but nothing I could compare to or learn from. I couldn't find any stories of people in my age range. Or people who are transgender. Or people who are suffering from lifelong depression. Or someone dealing with black sheep syndrome. I just felt like I was alone in this. I eventually got sick and tired of hearing the optimism from people who were not in my same position. I wanted to know I wasn't alone in this situation. I wanted to know that someone else had experienced the same thing and was able to bounce back from it.

If you're looking for the same thing, this is a read for you. You might not be dealing with a stroke; you may be experiencing a different major medical event. That's okay, this still could be a read for you. If you're struggling with childhood trauma and feel alone or you feel like you're in a helpless situation, this is a read for you. I don't claim to solve all your problems, but I wanted to tell my story in hopes that something in my story helps someone through their own struggle.

You are about to travel down a dark and rough road with me—the very road that I traveled. This road involves a lot of emotions and stories about those emotions. A lot of it is depression and there are discussions of suicidal thoughts. I wanted to share these stories to show people that emotions are very real and very normal, and even though we all have them, many fear them or don't understand their power. Emotions don't make you weak, and they aren't an illness. Processing your feelings and emotions is not something that should be looked down on. Regardless of whether we agree in life, with religious, or political views, we are all humans, and in the end, our hearts beat in a similar pattern. We all bleed red. We all have intrusive thoughts and emotions. Hopefully, you will see you're not alone, especially in troubled times. Someone out in this world is likely experiencing the same issues you're dealing with. Or they have experienced them. This world has a habit of making you feel like you are the only one with your problems, and that is a very lonely place to be. The truth is many others are experie-ncing the same thing. By today's standards, everyone has to look sparkly in the spotlight and their lives have to seem perfect, otherwise they aren't worth as much as others in society. We get embarrassed when people know our truths. You are about to hear my truths. You can choose your path from there. You can take what I've been through and use it to find strength in your own struggles, or you can write it off as something that happened to someone else. The choice is yours.

Now let's start our journey.

ABOUT ME
BS (BEFORE STROKE)

I think before I tell you my story, you should know more about me. I spent the first thirty-six years of my life thinking it was my fate to carry a dark cloud around with me. It seemed like Murphy's law was the one thing that I felt I could always count on in my life. Anything that could go wrong, would go wrong. I always felt like the universe was taunting me. I watched people get to live "normal", happy, successful lives. I say "normal" with quotations because like perfection, normal does not exist. People aren't "normal." You may have a "normal" life to you, but it may be different from others. There are all kinds and all types of human beings; different is the "normal" existence of humans. If you disagree, then we view the world very differently. Neither view is wrong, but neither of us are completely 100 percent right either. At least that's what I believe. Watching is what it always felt like—I could look but never touch or seem to reach that level in my life. I was always on the outside looking in.

As a child, I remember knowing that I was different from other little males. Some might say it's because I didn't have a father because he only lasted eighteen months after I was born. Others have their theories, but their theories meant nothing to me growing up and still mean nothing to me now. I know that I was born different. I was a young male who enjoyed singing along to The Little Mermaid and playing the Pink Ranger when we pretended to be the Power Rangers during recess. I wanted to hang around other males for more than just a "normal" friendship. When I was grouped with boys I felt out of place. Even at a young age, I was attracted to other males. When I was young, it wasn't sexual by any means; it was searching for an emotional connection, not for a romantic one, just a companion. Maybe I was looking for another person like me. I'm not sure though, because I never knew why I was different. From a young child I had always been in touch with my feminine side. To others, I was a "weird" little boy. I wasn't weird, I was just never like other boys. I spent a lot of time wondering why I related to Ariel so much and not Prince Eric. Some people feel shame because they find out someone they love is gay or trans. There is nothing you can do to avoid it. No amount of prayer or practice can stop people from being who they are. Your option to unconditionally love that person is controllable and a choice. Your opinion of them is a choice. Your respect for that person is also a choice. It is not possible to control who we really are. We shouldn't have to control or hide it. We should let it out. Being put in a closet is not real. Those who truly love you will be happy you're claiming your truth. That is what I prefer to call—what is often referred to as "coming out." No one "in a closet" chooses to be there. Coming out means we start "in." In should not be the default. There doesn't need to be a default that we diverge from. There are all kinds of different humans. We don't need to alienate those who have feelings beyond what society deems is normal or the default. Those who pretend to love you will question you. And you can pick who you want in your life or, as I refer to it, your village. It wasn't until my twenties that I discovered that family wasn't just blood and marriage. The greatest thing about LGBTQ+ people is that you are given the opportunity to choose your family. Your chosen family is your village. Chosen family is not reserved for the LGBTQ+ community, but it is seen often in our community because many of us are forced to be outcasts and outsiders from our own villages. So we often find people like us to substitute for those people. They don't always have labels; they are like-minded humans you're close to. They provide you something you're missing in your life. Chosen family helped me through a lot on this recovery. Much of my motivation to keep fighting was so I didn't let down my village.

Growing up, I had a mom, a stepfather, and two half brothers. My stepfather went from somewhat of a friend when I was much younger to completely shifting his attitude when my mom started having children with him. I was told we were inseparable in the early years of our relationship. I remember as a child, he would often take me to the store around the corner and treat me to a snack cake, or he would bring them home from work for me. He once took me fishing, and I remember having a bonding moment with him. It meant a lot to me because I knew I wasn't his child. A few years later, I dealt with the ultimate betrayal of a parent and was molested by that same man. After that, our relationship definitely changed. He began showing a lot of dislike for me. I personally believe that was his way of deflecting any suspicions. I think he believed if people saw that he disliked me, then why would he touch me. And in return, I developed a lot of hatred for him. I didn't like the shift from "friend" to foe, but it was a punch I had to roll with. One of many in my life. The constant name-calling and backhanded compliments were enough on their own, but everything together felt like daily torture.

So I believe because my home situation was mentally unhealthy for me, I looked for that healthy home feeling in other places. I was always a social butterfly but friendship carried far more weight to me than most others. Friends were very important to me. That happens when there is a bad home life. If I called you a friend, it was likely I would indeed take a bullet for you. In fact, I would get in trouble at school for being too social. In my preteens, I came to terms, somewhat, with who I was and claimed my truth of being a gay boy, this is because I never knew much about trans people. I say "somewhat" because my final evolution was to transition. I am now a transgender woman. This is not the normal progression for everyone that claims their truth as gay but transitioning was my truth. I found myself becoming far more in touch with my feminine side all the time. Through the years, I eventually resented the masculine parts of me. I decided that even though some would be uncomfortable, I needed to follow my path in the end.

A few years after being molested, when I was twelve, I met a few grown men with whom I was willing to learn more about myself with. I gave up my virginity to them, and like other men in my life that got what they wanted, they became very ugly with me, and eventually, they ghosted me altogether. Another fate I would deal with throughout my life—men ghosting me. Ugh. *#IYKYK* Since my birth, most of the men in my life have disappointed me and disappeared. The only man that ever stuck around was the one man I always wanted to disappear. That was a large factor in me believing I was meant to live a miserable life. I always felt bad for having those thoughts because it always felt selfish for wanting him gone, knowing my mom and brothers still had love for him and they would be hurt. They also didn't know what hurt I was hiding. I suppose I felt noble for keeping it a secret. I felt like I was keeping it a secret, but it also felt like everywhere I went, I carried a large teal balloon tied around my waist. This felt like everyone knew I was hiding a secret. It was a lot like keeping a secret that everybody could see. I couldn't imagine being the reason my brothers also grew up without a father. That feeling is the only reason I was ever nice to him; it wasn't out of respect for him—it was out of respect for the people I did love. In fact, I had then and still have zero respect for him and no trust either. This was all during a time when I didn't have the freedom to leave my home situation at will and find reprieve. At the time, the one person I could reach out to and feel comfortable to confide in, was my grandmother. This relationship was quite an issue with my own mom for several reasons. One of the first being my grandmother would say things and buy me things that my mom couldn't or wouldn't. I thought it was out of love, like a grandmother does. Later I found out that it was more like buying love. Looking back, it feels like recruitment. For what? I may never know. For a while, it worked. And why wouldn't it? This was when technology was just coming around as a necessity. Who didn't want a new cell phone or a computer? Especially a teenager. The other thing she offered was an ear. I felt like I could talk to her without judgment or ridicule. I didn't feel like my mom had my back like I expected her to. In situations where my stepfather and I would be at odds, I always felt like she took his side. I never hated my mom, but I would constantly compare her to my grandmother. My grandmother understood why I didn't want being at home. I felt like my mom was not reading the situation and was upset that I didn't want to be there. Another point of contention I believe was a little bit of jealousy from a young girl crying out, wanting to know why her mom treated others so much differently than her. She always felt like an outsider to her mom. My grandmother treated the men in the family like Gods amongst men. They could be doing or dealing drugs or they could be child molesters or women beaters, and she would give all but her skin for these men; and the younger, the more she would make you feel important. The girls in my grandmother's life always got treated like second-class citizens. A feeling I understood well because I felt that way with my stepfather. What did I do that made him hate me but still treat others so kindly? He would treat others so nicely, at least to their face. I even had friends who would tell me they liked him and that he was cool. When they'd say that, I would cringe. Looking back, I now believe it's because I held a secret that could shatter my family and ruin the reputation he thought he had. He always put on a face around new people in the hopes of looking better than he really was. Living with this arrogance was so frustrating. I had to learn to let him live his fantasy. If I didn't, my life would be much worse. It was stressful growing up in a house I often was very unhappy in, holding in a secret that disgusted me. I was struggling with my identity and then tragedy struck my family.

On top of everything else going on, I lost my aunt who I was very close to. My aunt Ruthanne was a "cool" aunt. She was twenty-five at the time and seemed to enjoy life for what it was. She would take up an entire room when she would enter it. I feel like if she were alive today, we would be best friends and nearly inseparable. She was so accepting of people for who they were. She was in a fatal car accident in 1997. She was the first person I truly loved that passed away. But if I was devastated, my mom was thoroughly destroyed. My mom grew up like a mother to her baby sister. They were best friends, sisters, and a little mother and daughter. Part of my mom died when my aunt did, so I lost my mom for a little bit too. We all dealt with a heavy loss at that time. I can honestly say my mom has a huge heart. She has a place in her heart for everyone she meets in life and even some she hasn't met. She has at least ten million places for her little sister. I don't remember exactly what happened, but I remember feeling a distance between her and the world after that. When she wasn't in bed, she was on autopilot, going through work and life. It made me feel weird because I was angry that my mom was not as present as before; even though she was still in front of us, her spirit just seemed drained. Not like an energy drain that could be restored over a good night's sleep. The kind of drained that requires repair. The house was filled with sadness and sorrow for a long time. I was filled with anger and confusion. Anger because I wanted my mom back and confusion because I also felt bad for being angry because she was in such pain. It was the first event that had caused me that much pain, but I seemed to recover fairly quickly. My world stabilized, and even though there was something missing, I was able to continue growing and getting through. I was jaded, thinking I had experienced the worst feelings this life can cause. Boy, was I wrong.

There was a lot of healing in that house happening after that. My childhood was spent looking for the kind of family you'd only see on TV or in movies. I knew our family was not conventional but neither were the Tanners or the Lamberts, and they got along fine. I just wanted that kind of family with that kind of love. Maybe my expectations of a family were too cliché, but I wanted a father that was wise and protective. I wanted my mother to be in a healthy relationship that I could learn from. For a while, it seemed like we were all a little closer, and as nice as that was, there was always a reminder in the back of my mind to not get too close to the enemy. I spent my preteens looking for myself and my truth. I decided that I needed to be my true self, and I claimed my truth. I quickly lost respect for people who acted like I was letting them down for being gay. Learning how to take back my respect for people helped me care much less than I used to about how they felt about me. I personally found that having no respect for someone often stops me from being affected by their feelings about me. I later heard that ideology put into words, which made it so much easier for me to make sense of this idea and not care about others' opinions. RuPaul once said, "Other people's opinions of me are none of my business!" I'll carry that advice with me forever. I spent my teen years looking for lifelong friends. I wanted friends like the ones in *Saved by the Bell* or *Boy Meets World*, friends I could grow with that I would know inside and out. My brothers were four and six years younger than me, so on top of having a completely different set of growing pains to process, we also were far apart in the type of family dynamics we were growing up in. I figured it would be easier to relate to people my own age. Much to my dismay, the friendships I made would bloom and wilt like an unwatered flower. Meaning, as quickly as I would start and grow a new friendship was also how long it took that friendship to die.

A memory that always sticks out is about friends, or lack thereof, when I graduated my senior year of high school basically alone. My family was in the audience, and I knew they were proud of me and likely surprised, but I watched countless others celebrating their friends' achievements after the ceremony, and I was walking out of graduation by myself. A very disappointing event indeed. Only weeks before my Graduation, I had what I thought was a solid group of friends. graduation felt like being a part of a Saved by the Bell episode, but I had a very minor role and no lines. It was great to be celebrated by my family, but there is no feeling like being around those who survived the battle with you.

We often get told as high school students to stay in school and the dropout rates got thrown in our faces constantly. We were fully aware how our lives could turn out if we were to quit or fail high school. Every day that we walked out of school felt like another day had been survived. Especially after what was considered the last good year (1998). I once heard a story about how 1998 was the last good year in most millennials' lives. I agree with this theory, so I'll tell you about it.

As young people in America, we watched TV, but the news was not most young teenagers' preference. Although I knew a guy in high school who watched more news than his parents. As you can tell from my earlier references, I liked feel-good shows. It was good to know what kind of events were taking place in the world, but we weren't interested in tragedies; even then we were chasing the nostalgic feelings of cereal and Saturday morning cartoons. We tried holding onto the security of our younger years.

For many millennials, 1998 was like our last good year or our last tragedy-free year. There were tragedies prior to 1998 but nothing like what came after. We had heard the stories of Rodney King, the riots, O. J. Simpson, and Jon Benét Ramsey. These stories brought up feelings of concern because it had proven to younger people that there was evil in the world. Even though some of us already knew that. But there was distance between us and those victims we could relate to, but for most, there was no direct connection to those victims. It made it easier to separate yourself from those tragedies. It also brought to light the problems with our society. As long as you were paying attention. Hindsight being 20/20 you can tell what millennials were paying attention and which ones were coasting through. As a middle schooler going to high school next year, the Columbine High School massacre shook me to my fucking core. In middle school, the problems and the bullies were bigger than in elementary school. I could only figure the problems and bullies would grow exponentially from middle school to high school. My struggles at home, my struggles of a "gay" boy's coming of age, and now my fears everyday of just going to school, it's no wonder I couldn't focus. Every day the bus arrived at school, it felt like I was being delivered to the slaughterhouse. Every time I saw a student upset, I wondered if tomorrow was gonna be the day a student would become unhinged and want to start shooting. Every time a fight broke out, was someone gonna pull a gun? No one knew. Until then school felt like a safe place. From then on, I tried to remain as observant and diligent as possible at all times. Well, the next event could not be missed.

The Y2K panic didn't require diligence to know about it. It happened fast and with almost no warning. Someone was loud enough to catch the ear of the media and mass hysteria ensued. People thought money was just going to disappear and computers controlling bombs would fail and end the world. People thought technology was going to end civilization as we knew it. The panic spread like the most dangerous game of Telephone ever played. As teenagers, we watched otherwise sane adults, who we trusted, lose their minds. NYE 2000 came and went. The world was still here. Computers didn't explode or just flatline; the only booming we heard were the fireworks and people partying, welcoming the new millennium.

The next majorly stressful event was terror hitting in one of the worst ways. September 11th was terrifying for the whole world, and we all had our own experiences and damages caused by it. Even if we weren't directly involved, it had effects on us. When it passed this year, twenty-two years later, I heard tons of stories of people who recounted their experiences from that day. Here's mine... I was in ninth grade, and I was on my way to my health class. I felt a feeling in the air that day. An ominous feeling. Later, I saw that some teachers were acting strange. There were several teachers trying to hold back their feelings, but you could see something was wrong; either something was very wrong or every teacher had indigestion at the exact same time that day. They all looked like they were holding back whatever they could. Some were shaking, some were in tears, all of them exhibiting emotions that caused me to notice. I remember I stood still for a minute and listened for commotion. Was this the day? I didn't hear gunshots or screaming, so I assumed it was all clear and continued to class. I sat at my desk and pulled out my notebook for health. I hoped that class would resume as usual. I sat there waiting to hear more about sexually transmitted diseases before it was changed to sexually transmitted infections, and the uneasy feeling grew more and more powerful. A student suddenly burst through the door and told my health teacher that a second plane crashed in the World Trade Center. Questions immediately started forming: 1) What was the World Trade Center? I knew it was in New York, so I assumed it was a skyscraper. 2) Why was a pilot flying a plane by New York low enough to hit a skyscraper? 3) Why was everyone freaking out over a stupid accident? She quickly turned the TV on and turned it to the news, and we all watched. I quickly got my questions answered. We watched the planes hit repeatedly because it was on replay on every news channel. We knew there were people on the planes and people in the buildings. I didn't know who to feel more sorry for. Neither situation seemed like the lesser of two evils. I could only imagine the terror those victims experienced. I watched people jump from the buildings, choosing their own fate. We watched the buildings crash to the ground, burying others. I kept wondering how someone could do this. How could this even happen? And then they told us that it was not an accident. Terrorists took over planes to crash them into the buildings. That made imagining the terror much worse. It was all to prove a point. The point was that they could. The security of our country was suddenly a fallacy. It felt like nothing was secure at that time. There were plenty of theories behind the attacks, but no one could say for sure then. There's still people who don't know exactly what or why it happened. You could tell teachers were doing their best to stay calm, but you could feel the fear in the air. Words like *terror, tragedy, casualties*, and *violence* all had more intense meanings suddenly. We weren't perm-anently destroyed as a country, but we were definitely shaken. For me, I had just learned the hard way that not everyone thought of America like America did. I can confidently say that 9/11 had an effect on me. What exactly the effect was may always be a mystery but witnessing thousands of lives extinguished and unknown amounts more damaged or shattered has an impact on a person. After the Columbine massacre, fear was different. After Y2K, panic was different, and after 9/11, terror was different. Life was different from that point on. I feel like the effects these events had on a person halfway through the growth process were enough to impact an entire generation. It's hard to believe that many assumed there would be no repercussions on people that would be long lasting. I think that as most of us were just getting our first taste of the real world, we expected a safe and nurturing world like many children had experienced in their home lives. But we were met at the door to reality with uncertainty, people who were capable of things beyond our nightmares, and the discovery that our lives are fragile and we really don't control them. Life came at us very fast after that. I'm sure that out of all these tragedies something good was born. At the very least, a generation wanted to bring mental health to focus. For some, the lives saved were not worth the lives lost. But normalizing mental health awareness is an amazing thing. People are not just "crazy" anymore. There are treatments for things now that before would just get you thrown in an asylum. That's just the opinion of someone who lived through life after "the last good year." My younger years were really spent just surviving life. I felt like there was no escape from what life threw at me until later. I honestly wasn't going to college. My family was never going to be able to afford it, and my grades were not the kind of grades that warranted a scholarship. My option was to work after high school. So I did. low-paying jobs were all I could land. I still lived at home. It was embarrassing to talk to friends about my home life because I was an "adult," so that meant I had no one to turn to when my stepfather's torment would be raging. My mom's advice was to simply ignore him, which was a difficult task when he's screaming at you in the face. Especially after we had been in a physical fight before. This man would throw world-ending fits about shampoo bottles being empty, and if the blinds in the living room were closed, the house looked like "a fucking morgue," and he'd angrily open the blinds. Then if the blinds were open, he didn't want "the fucking neighbors to see what we were doing in our house," and he would angrily slam them closed. I was not dealing with two smart parents like most; he was like a grown eight-year-old. My mom was very smart and taught me a lot about life, but I will never understand why I was always the one told to "Be the bigger person". In fact, I often got told not to fight with him because I was much smarter. There was no way to please him. He would make sure we got ice cream for dessert after every meal, then he would try to make me feel bad by calling me fat and telling me that one day I would explode. If a glass sat on the table for even a second after you swallowed the last drop, the house was a "fucking mess" and "dirty dishes belong in the fucking sink!" And he would snatch the glass and throw it in the sink. But if you put in the sink, he couldn't understand why we went through so many "fucking dishes" while throwing dishes around in the sink to make sure you knew he meant business. The torment from my stepfather continued as long as I was there. I don't know why I assumed things would change as an adult, but they never did. Then people wondered why I turned to drinking. A deep analysis of the way I feel about my childhood concludes that a lot of my drinking problems were a trauma response.

MY FIRST ESCAPE

BS (BEFORE STROKE)

So, when I finally got the chance to get out of my childhood home, I jumped at the opportunity. A friend of mine from high school reconnected with me, and we eventually became roommates. It was a terribly sad and an extremely happy day all the same. I didn't want to leave my mom or my brothers, but I didn't have the energy to deal with my stepfather anymore. To avoid the tears, I cleared out while everyone was gone.

I had contemplated suicide in my teens from my stepfather's torment alone. I could never follow through with it because I always felt like I had a reason to stay here. Something always told me I was meant for more than unhappiness and to be misunderstood. Maybe there was something bigger in my future, but also, maybe it was my sheer dislike for my stepfather that wouldn't let me end my misery and allow him to continue on. Either way, me getting rid of myself made it seem like he would win, and that would never happen. Either way, this felt like an escape to me. Between the confusion of who I was, the treatment at home, the mind fuckery of the recent years—I just wanted it all to stop. So I felt like removing myself from the biggest catalyst of the negativity in life was the best option. I can remember feeling relief from his torment, but I also remember feeling new kinds of stress from adulting. My new stress was no comparison to the way I had felt before. It didn't matter too much because that time away didn't last long, and I had to return back to my childhood home, where the torment continued. My friend and I chose to share a one-bedroom apartment. We shared the one bedroom and had both of our beds in it. It seemed like a great idea initially, but we soon found out the close quarters were too close. I was forced to move back; it felt like I was destined to fail my whole life. I was approaching my twenties, my job was minimum wage, I was not going to college, and I was driving a POS. I was always hoping for my storm cloud to break. I just wanted a chance to succeed.

My twenties were spent trying to grow out of that shell of a broken child and figure out this whole adulting bullshit. I assumed while growing up, certain things just happened. A good job was waiting for me, good credit would just happen one day, and my prince was always around the corner or at the other end of the crowded bar. I figured at some age, these things just appeared. They did for others—gay or straight, fat or thin—but never for me. I felt like I was being too shy and playing it too coy. So I began throwing myself at every man who looked at me. However, none of them cared. Maybe they smelled the desperation, or maybe they just weren't attracted. Either way, my feelings were never reciprocated. When I'd finally catch someone's eye, it always felt like something was starting. I'd anticipate good things and wait for the romance to start but would continue to be disappointed, and the men would disappear. Everyone around me managed to stumble into relationships, and I couldn't catch one with a net.

All I knew was I had nothing but love, support, and companionship for the man that wanted it. Much of my twenties were spent proving to myself that I am worthy of love, even if I was a flamboyant drag queen, who was overweight and didn't have the nicest things in life. You can see how I felt about myself. I figured if I wasn't good enough for a good partner, a good job, or good credit, I must not be good enough for society. The rest of my twenties were spent looking for love. I spent my thirties reassessing my life and trying to rebuild what I had fucked up in my teens and twenties. I got myself into a new career, traveled the country a little, fixed my credit a little, and I started putting the pieces together to form a life where I was finally adulting. It didn't matter because, after years of trying to improve my credit, it was still on the low side. I was making decent money but I felt I had nothing to show for it. I had a vehicle, I had an apartment, I had money. I wasn't worried when I went to grocery store or the gas pump. I felt successful in my own way. But compared to societal standards, I was still a failure. My past failures would continue to follow and haunt me for many years. I remember the day I was offered my first professional job. I was so excited, and I just knew life would improve. It did...for a few years. My new career had landed me a job in Pennsylvania. Having lived in Michigan my whole life, I was excited to leave and experience a different place. I don't know if it was the same for everyone, but my hometown seemed to have a hook in me, and I was always tethered to this place. When I left Michigan, I was excited, confident, and optimistic. I eventually had to quit my job because I was not seeing eye to eye with my boss. When I returned to Michigan, I felt defeated once again. I felt my optimism turn to pessimism, and I felt like I ruined the best opportunity I ever had. I was filled with regret. I couch hopped for three weeks and was then offered a better role in Tennessee. I left again to a new place, and with each mile closer to my new home, my optimism returned. In true hometown fashion, my new home was temporary—again. This time, I had no backup and couch hopping wasn't an option. My options were homelessness or back to my childhood home again As unwelcome as I felt, I chose a roof. I loved my new rescue dog, and I couldn't have him living in a car, so I sacrificed my own happiness. Little did

I know it would be a new chapter in the same old book—more stress and unnecessary torment. I suppose part of me knew that was going to be the case, but I was hoping for something a little different. When I had to go home again, I didn't expect a red carpet, but I expected a little more sympathy than I got. I figured that there would be some more empathy; instead, it felt like I was being pushed a little more each day to leave. I just assumed that there would be a little more understanding for someone who just lost one of the best jobs they've ever had. I barely was given time to process what happened. I started a new job, working from home, and was able to pick up a lot of my pieces.

Suddenly, my ministroke hit, and it felt like another blow to my life; more about this soon. I wondered if my body was giving up on me. Shortly after, I finally got approved for an apartment and was able to get away from that huge catalyst of my stress once again. I got set up in my new apartment, and things felt hopeful again.

A WAY BACK TO THEN

In the year leading up to my major stroke, I was laid off from my work-from-home job—thanks, COVID—and was forced to get unemployment for a while, which was far less than my income was previously. Bills started falling behind and things started looking bleak again. I woke up every day expecting an eviction notice on my door or my car being gone from in front of my apartment. My stress levels were so high. I would be in an intense depression one day, and the next day, the depression would be bearable. My anxiety would have me all over the map. I had no solid outlet or healthy outlet anyway. As the stress and pressure grew heavier and heavier, I found myself drinking more and more again. My give-a-damn was busted. Maybe my drinking was a coping mechanism. Maybe it was me trying to go back to a time when I felt like royalty and things seemed to not be as difficult or as serious. You know the secret to time travel is at the bottom of a whiskey bottle, didn't you? It really isn't, but I thought it was.

In my twenties, I frequented a bar where everyone knew me and most loved me. On my twenty-first birthday there, I had twenty shots bought for me. When I walked up and there was a line to get in on a Friday night, I could skip it and walk right up to the door. I never paid for cover, and when bartenders saw me approaching, my drink would be ready for me when I got to the bar. I was often told that I kept the lights on in the bar. When I went outside for a cigarette, the cigarettes were offered to me like offerings to a queen, and I never lit my own. I missed those days because I felt loved and embraced. Things didn't feel as real as they did now. But also, those days got me in trouble a lot. That royalty wasn't real. Most of those people who "loved me" were nowhere to be found in my hard times. This experience was no different. As my drinking increased, so did my need for new feelings. I started snorting coke when it was available where I was; I was hoping that my life would go back to a time when I was truly happy. Well, at least I felt truly happy, but that was likely a cognitive distortion due to the alcohol. With the increased alcohol consumption and the new cocaine usage, I found myself having a lot of sex. I was embracing my new feminine features, and men were noticing me, typically when I was drunk, sometimes high. And I wanted to feel really good. I may never know where my mind was at, but these were not my usual behaviors. I was abusing myself and letting others abuse me. For a while, my life felt like I was in a fast car, running red lights, not caring about the oncoming traffic. I was driving, but I had no control. I was trying to hold it all together as best as I could, and this major stroke hit, and I fell apart like one of those toys where you push the bottom button and the toy collapses into pieces. This experience was no different. I tell you all this for two major reasons. The first one is that I was never really a happy person for most of my life. I always felt like someone had placed a curse on me. I began exhibiting behaviors of someone who was crying out for help. But no one could hear me or no one cared enough. I was already mentally in a terrible place from the last thirty-six years of living to survive, and I had a past filled with trauma that haunted me constantly. The second reason I told you all this about me is because I will reference all of it a little later, and the transparency will help make more sense of everything.

MY STROKES
(MY MAJOR STROKE)

I woke up on Friday, January 13, 2023, not feeling right. I thought I might have been having a high blood pressure episode of some kind. The feeling was foreign but also ominously familiar. I had felt this feeling once before. My head felt light and my legs felt weak.

But there was something new this time. My vision was absolutely wild; it was like someone was pranking me. The right side of my vision looked completely normal, but the left side looked like someone bled all the color out of my world. It was 100 percent black and white. I'm talking about the early I Love Lucy years. This immediately made me think something was going on with my brain. I texted a friend, and she urged me to go to the hospital. Well, actually, she told me to call 9-1-1. I chose to drive myself. I took my dog out to use the bathroom, put my shoes on, and left my apartment to drive myself to the ER. I could have never predicted that that would be the last time my world felt "normal" or the last time I would be waking up in that apartment. Or that I wouldn't see my dog for the better part of a year or longer. Or that my entire life would be turned upside down and inside out. As I drove to the ER, I felt like I was driving fine. I even used my left hand to smoke a cigarette—another last for me. I got to the ER, and they told me that they think I've had a stroke. They had suspicions of that the last time too.

MY STROKES
(MY MINISTROKE)

In October of 2021, I had eaten three edibles and fell asleep. When I woke up, the right side of my body was weak, and I was extremely lightheaded. I went to the ER three times in three days and spent nearly thirteen hours in the waiting room. Thanks again COVID. Because all my limbs were working but the right side seemed extremely weakened, they focused on the lightheaded symptom. They recommended a drug similar to Dramamine, diagnosed me with viral vertigo, and recommended I stay at the hospital until Monday. It was a Saturday. They wanted the neurologist to assess me. That meant at least two overnight stays in the hospital. Prior to that, I had a friend who had a medical emergency that sent him to the hospital for two weeks, and his bill was around $23,000. I was so stressed about leaving with a bill like that when I could barely pay all my bills in general. I left the hospital against medical recommendation and went back to my childhood bedroom, where I had been living with my huge dog. I was on the brink of a mental breakdown because I felt I had finally started getting my life together after one of the worst experiences until that point. I had been moving around to different states as a property manager. I had been let go from my last job in Tennessee coincidentally after disclosing to one of my bosses that I was looking to transition. I was congratulated and then let go a few days later supposedly because I was doing my job poorly. I will never be convinced that that was true because I was the only person keeping that property together. I am not one to cry prejudice but this situation felt ironically coincidental. But you know my Murphy's law theory, so I guess it had to happen. Anything that could go wrong, would go wrong. At least that's how I always felt. Of course, I would lose my job when things were going well. That has happened my whole life. Or at least it felt like that. Things would go to shit when things started going well, or what I perceived as things going well. I had to move back to not only my home state but also my childhood home, a place where I was typically miserable. The worst part is, I felt like I was not at all welcome there. I felt extremely unwelcome, especially in such a devastating time of my life. My mental health was on the edge. What's worse is I was once again living in the same home, in the same room, with the same man who had tormented me for years. There were memories there I just wanted to forget, but instead, I was reminded of them every night. I felt like my life was falling apart. When I got back to my old/new bedroom from leaving the emergency room, I looked up strengthening techniques for the limbs and joints I had weaknesses in. I practiced writing my name because my handwriting had gotten very messy due to weakness in my right hand; I wrote my name over and over again like a schoolchild in trouble, writing sentences I practiced putting my right flip-flop on using only my foot because my toes were no longer flexing like normal. I practiced walking when I could and eventually strengthened those limbs enough to be nearly back to normal. I was not able to wear high heels anymore because my ankle was still not as strong as it was before. But also, I'm six feet four, I don't really need heels. I was working on this though. If I would've had adequate insurance when they asked me to stay at the hospital, or I hadn't been struggling financially, and I wouldn't have been terrified of the financial repercussions, I would've stayed for the neurologist to do the MRI on me, and I would've found out that it was a stroke the first time. They could have treated me for the health factors that contributed to the first stroke, and I could have been informed of how to potentially prevent a second one. But because I felt the American health-care system focuses on money and not medical health, I was immediately anxious about the bill, and I chose to put my health on the back burner. I made the decision to leave, but the idea of a huge bill terrified me. Just an FYI, those three ER visits landed me with a bill of over $8,000. After months of phone calls, endless sleepless nights, and applications for help, I finally got that bill paid. I convinced myself that I would be okay and could go home. When people asked what happened, I told them I had a ministroke. I had no idea that my jokes about my ministroke were true! I wouldn't find out that they were true until my MRI—the one I had in 2023– showed that there were two lesions on my brain. One on the right, which affected the left side of my body, and one on the left side of my brain, which affected the right side of my body. Since my right side was working fine now, they assumed the lesion was caused by the first stroke in 2021. In all honesty, I thought my body had a weird reaction to the edibles back then. I had no idea what happened, and I had never looked up what a stroke is or what it does to the body. I had no idea what kind of effects it had on us. I honestly thought if you had a stroke, it basically meant death. I also thought that strokes happened to people much older than thirty-six. I thought they only happened to older bodies that were worn out. It was not a normal topic of conversation, so I didn't know how to detect a problem early on. There weren't any signs by the way. I had never spent time discussing deadly ways your body can betray you. I also didn't know how to work toward preventing it. I didn't know that my blood pressure, my blood sugar, my smoking, my estrogen injections, my weight, my cholesterol, and my eating and drinking habits were all contributing to a soon-to-be tragedy.

Some might think the word "tragedy" is dramatic. I've heard people say, "At least you're alive!" They were right, I was alive, but I felt like the living dead for a long time. I felt like I was meant to die, and for some reason, my body refused. To me, it was a true tragedy. It was beyond difficult to take in. Between the new physical limitations and the mental toll, I felt like I would never be like the old me again. It felt like all that was left for me was for my body to break down, and it would be the end. I didn't feel like recovering was possible.

I started looking up stroke stories and learned it was possible to recover; however, the uncertainty of recovering from any brain injury is out of control. The uncertainty for any recovery is out of control. Some recover fully, some recover partially, some never recover at all. How did I know what category I was in? I didn't and some immediate differences had me questioning my ability to recover. One of the worst things was the way my brain would tire so quickly. I mean, watching TV in my room with my overhead light on would wear me out. With my light on and the sound of the emergency room was close to torture. Reading a text felt like reading the Constitution. My past history of bad luck kept reminding me that I was in a hopeless situation. Thinking back to the good times or the good experiences or the time I spent with my niece and nephew just made me sad, so I stopped thinking about those times! I don't place the blame on the hospital for allowing me to leave because that was my choice, but I look back at that moment with regret. If I would've stayed in the hospital for only three or four days, I could have maybe avoided a nightmare that lasted for 11 months. But the balance to this nightmare was a personal rebirth that helped me look at life through a different lens. The best way to get out of a terrible situation is through it, right? At least that's what some say and I had a lot to go through.

THE FEELING OF FADING

After they said it might be a stroke, they laid me down in a bed in the ER, and that was when my life began changing. Until then I had full control over everything. I even made sure to check because of my experience the first time. My fingers and toes all functioned correctly. I checked because of the last time I felt this feeling. As I laid there, and the blood clot in my brain continued to do damage to me beyond my comprehension and without my knowledge. It was like being attacked by a close friend behind your back. As the blood clot cut off my blood supply to the right side of my brain, the left side of my body began to fade away. At least it felt like fading.

I can't remember the exact order, but at one point,

one of the doctors asked me to squeeze both of their hands with mine. Only the right hand was able to reach out and squeeze her hand. The left arm was bent toward my body, and my hand curled up like it was a slug that someone poured salt on. I didn't know what that meant, and I immediately feared the worst for my situation. That started me off in a mindset spent thinking about the doom and gloom. I was already nervous about the repercussions of this medical incident—physically, mentally, and monetarily. These feelings made it all worse. At another point, I had to get up and pee. When I tried standing up, I discovered my left leg was no longer functional. This was devastating to me, more than I knew at the time. I went from being fully capable and independent to being fully dependent on help to do anything at all in what felt like minutes.

I remember, after, they scolded me for not asking for help—a scolding that was bullshit because this was not something that was explained to me. At that point, they had not yet confirmed a stroke. They assumed I was just supposed to know that I could no longer walk. I didn't realize that that was the first of many occasions I would just need to know things, and things were not explained properly to me. When they were done scolding me, they handed me a handheld urinal. As I relieved myself in my bed, I felt my dignity start fading away. I was terrified to know how I would poop. I had never not been able to walk to the bathroom. Terrified was a gross understatement of how I was feeling. Not just for the bathroom, but I walked into the emergency room and to the bed I was lying on. What was happening to me? I tried to stay positive and optimistic because no one was calling a code blue for my room, but fear was quickly taking over everything. Every thought. Every word. Every breath. I had never been in a situation like this. I remember holding my bowel movement for as long as I could to avoid any further humiliation. All that did was cause them to slip me MiraLAX. That just made things worse because at that point, it had been days I was admitted to the hospital. They then gave me a call light for help and placed me in an adult diaper, referred to as a brief, for vanity purposes. Hitting that call light to get help often meant a ten-minute or more wait for help, which sometimes meant a diaper change or worse.

Some people came to visit me in the ER, and I remember smelling the cold January air on them. I was jealous and felt as though I was being held captive. I lay in bed as the dawn turned to day, and I was becoming inpatient. I wanted nothing more than to go home. I wanted to pet my dog, and I wanted to feel normal again. Me wanting to know when I would be discharged was a recurring question during this recovery. When the doctor said they were going to admit me for testing, I was instantly discouraged that I would be going home anytime soon. The future didn't hold that in my cards. The universe had other plans for me.

By the time I got admitted, the stroke had taken its full effect. I suddenly needed help with everything. I even needed help to move in bed! like rolling over. I remember wanting to give up on life. The effects were taking place, and the initial shock was wearing off as I learned what being a stroke patient in the hospital meant. Life had punched me in the gut a million times and then kicked me when I was down; it was a poetic ending to a tragic life, right? I remember feeling absolutely worthless at this time. This was when I remember questioning if I would live through this. I also remember asking the universe what the point of keeping me alive was. I asked what the point was of me surviving a near-fatal stroke just to be a bedridden human, needing help with everything.

As I talked to the universe, a nurse came into my room with meds. I was sobbing from my conversation with the universe, and the nurse held my hand. She said, "Meetri'a, why are you crying?" Her voice was kind, caring, and filled with concern. Plus, she used my preffered name. She said my name as if I was always Meetri'a. Hearing your proffered name like that is absolute magic. I felt safe with this woman, so I confided in her. I told her I asked the universe what the point of keeping me alive was for me to feel like I did every day. I woke up feeling like I was an inconvenience and a lost cause being kept alive because I refused to die. She made eye contact with me and wiped the tears from my eyes. She then said, "I don't know the reason why you are still alive, but please, know there was a reason, I promise." She was not anything other than a human nurse, but something about what she said and the way she said it was like a spoonful of sugar for my soul. It made that day a little bit more bearable, and it would give me a purpose, and that was to find a purpose. If there was a reason for my life to be spared, I had to find it if for no other reason than to know why my life was worth saving.

Early on, I remember having thoughts of me dying being easier for me and everyone around me. My funeral planning may have been an easier time on the phone than me on the other end of the line crying and carrying on about all kinds of shit. It was about as morbid a thought as one could have, but it was realistic. I couldn't imagine how others were affected by what was happening to me or what I was doing to them with my constant crying and phone calls filled with despair. I had a best friend going through some medical issues of her own, and I'm sure what happened to me didn't make her feel any better about her own health. My mother had been surviving colon cancer for years, and in her weakened state, she couldn't be with me. I'm sure she was experiencing her own torment on top of dealing with her own mortality. I didn't know how my medical dilemma impacted others. Some felt obligated to come see me, others didn't. Some cared enough to at least reach out. Others waited for me to reach out to them. The last thing on my mind was finding the strength in me to fight my negative thoughts and my fears of what my future held to reach out to others and hold a meaningful conversation. I was consumed with fears of the future, embarrassment of my situation, worries of overwhelming those helping me, and the impending financial issues to follow. My vehicle was up for repossession, and my apartment was heading toward eviction status, and that was even before the stroke. I felt like I was going to need to rebuild my entire life again, only this time, at almost forty years old. The situation appeared hopeless at first glance. I have dealt with depression and feelings of loneliness my whole life, but this time, things got much worse. The loneliness felt more like abandonment, and the depression became almost visible. It could be a beautiful sunny day outside, but in my room, I was surrounded by rain clouds and fog. It was worse than I ever experienced when I was younger.

A dipiction of how I was feeling.

MY NEW TEMPORARY HOME

I went from being in the ER to being admitted to a hospital room for several days to an inpatient rehabilitation at a different hospital for around a month into a nursing home that offers rehabilitation services for the rest of my time on the inside. Yes, the inside. It felt like I was living in my own personal prison or within the walls of *M. Night Shyamalan's The Village*. The world advanced around me but every day was still that Friday in January, and I was trying to wake up from the worst dream. I cried every day for at least the first month of my stay at the nursing home. The vibes here were not good vibes of healing and recovery. The vibes here were vibes of despair, hopelessness, and death. I started contemplating suicide again. Again, the thoughts of giving up stopped me. I felt again that I was meant for so much more than this life bedridden, post-stroke life. I have experienced people at the end of their lives, and they often know when it's their time. As often as I've had suicidal thoughts, I've always found a reason not to go through with it, and I have never felt like it was my time yet. I returned to a feeling I knew well. I returned to feeling worthless, and I felt like I was fighting for basic things, like using the bathroom and not a bedpan. I found myself finding the will often to set goals for myself and then get therapy to help me reach those goals. If you'd like to feel less than human, please try using a bedpan or wearing an adult brief that you're expected to use the bathroom in when no one is available to put you on a bedpan. Every time I got on the bed pan or had someone wipe my butt or every time someone gave me a bed bath, my dignity would deteriorate little by little, and eventually, I felt like I had none at all. I was told by an aide once, "You always have to poop at the worst times!" like I chose when I wanted to poop. Sometimes these people don't think before opening their mouths. I coundn't control anything, and I felt like I was being ridiculed for things I couldn't control. I was often treated like a nursing care patient, not a rehab patient. In fact, it was proven when I had a discussion with someone who said to me,

"I treat all of the patients the same." They said.

"That's the problem, you can't talk to everyone in here the same. People here have all different levels of comprehension and faculties. Talking to everyone the same means you are not being respectful to the kind of care they need." I replied.

A rehab patient wants to test their boundaries and see what they can and can't do. At least I did. That treatment alone was a source of darkness that made it easier for my depression to sneak in and take over. The sadness was so overwhelming for such a long time. I spent so much time remembering what I had before, feeling like I would never get any of it back and comparing it to what I have now. I had gone from waking up next to my one-hundred-pound puppy,

walking out of my apartment to my car and driving myself to get some Starbucks and then go searching for a new job. Now I was waking up in a foreign bed, usually to someone I didn't know, asking me to eat a breakfast I didn't like or want. I was forced to trade in my music every morning for the sounds of call button alarms ringing annoyingly loud. Or screams of pain from nearby patients. I traded in fighting opponents on Fortnite every night with friends, my brother, and my nephew to fighting with CNAs who were supposedly here to help me, but instead, it felt like they found more fulfillment in seeing how long I would wait to use the bedpan before reaching my boiling point and start yelling at them that *"I'm going to shit my bed!"*
What an embarrassing direction my life had gone. I traded in my toilet for a bedpan and a handheld urinal. I traded in my California king-size memory foam bed for a nine-inch-thick jailhouse mattress. I traded in sleeping next to my dog for a pillow to prop up my left arm.

Even though I was in a state of depression in the months leading up to my stroke, I was still pushing forward because I was finally claiming my truth as a transwoman, and I already had new experiences to look forward to. I was riding the high of living my real truth, so I tried to remember that in my low moments. Men also started noticing me. I was surprised but also not. I had heard that a lot of men have a hidden thing for trans girls. I was happy for the attention either way. Especially so when my behavior was going off the rails. I used that attraction to continue behaving badly. I felt like something had to go my way eventually, so I pressed on through the dark times, looking for those moments of light. Every time I thought I was getting close to finding it, it felt like the universe screamed "Psych!" and pulled it away. I would be devastated for a little bit, and finally my spirits would rise and, with it, a new day to conquer. I would feel so strong and ready to make my dreams come true. Then depression would hit, and the new day looked gloomy and gross. I was on an emotional roller coaster. Then this stroke came crashing into my life like the Kool-Aid man into someone's living room. After the initial shock came months of agonizing discomfort. I wasn't experiencing pain in my body. My brain could only process so much before I was so tired that I needed to sleep. I was bored senseless and would want company, but company was also so hard to handle. If it wasn't my exhaustion, I had to use the bathroom or got uncomfortable and had to be moved in bed. People often felt compelled to leave; nothing felt normal anymore. I remember one day, I was lying in bed, and it was raining very hard. Droplets pounded against my window, which was strange because it was cold and snowy outside. It felt like a message from the universe, and suddenly, a movie quote came to mind. In *V for Vendetta*, Evey said, "God is in the rain," while having a serious emotional breakthrough. I am not a firm believer of religion, and I don't practice any kind of religion. I believe in the universe and, now more importantly, the balance of the universe. The universe is just as mysterious as God. I have the hardest time believing there is some vengeful man sitting in the clouds, conducting the world like a symphony. I believe the universe puts things in our paths that we need at the time. Maybe the universe thought I needed a break after exhibiting signs of spiraling, or maybe I was heading toward something beyond repair. At least I now know that this stroke is something I can repair and recover from with motivation and hard work. A drug charge, a disease, a third DUI, or worse could be things that could have ruined me beyond repair. I am not saying those are things that are guaranteed to ruin a person, but with where I was mentally, a stroke was maybe the most survivable outcome. After watching the rain outside falling and hearing large heavy drops hitting the window, I began repeating to myself, "God is in the rain." I was hoping for my breakthrough. I wanted the weight of this depression to lift. I remember pleading to the rain, asking to be restored to my normal self. I then apologized for believing in the universe and not God. I then said, "Well, if you are real, you created the universe. And since I believe in the power of the universe, I guess I believe in you by proxy." Since there was no beam of light and no vision that came to me, reassuring me that I was right or wrong, I continued to put my faith in the guidance of the universe. Putting my faith in the universe was how I realized that that helped me out of my depression and through this recovery.

I vividly remember saying to myself that this stroke was not fair. I then recalled saying that as a child and being told, "Well, life isn't fair!" But true fairness is balance and balance is something that is guaranteed no matter what your faith is in. They all talk about where there is darkness, there is light; where there is good, there is evil. So while it may not seem fair at the time, maybe what you're experiencing is your life balancing out. Maybe my life was going off the rails because I was giving up. I was doing so much to destroy my life that I needed to be put down for a while, but the universe knew I wasn't ready to be done, so it chose a different path. There was more for me. Maybe the universe wanted me to calm down and knew I wouldn't do it on my own, and I needed a forced break. A forced detox. A reset. Maybe the first ministroke was a warning, but it wasn't enough to get me to realize I was heading down a detrimental path. Maybe I lost certain jobs because I had learned the lessons I needed to learn from those jobs. Maybe I was forced back into my childhood home not to continue to be miserable but to deal with my traumas. Maybe the universe wanted me to stop repressing things and face them head-on.

I may never be given a definitive answer, but I've learned to look at situations differently. I used to put situations in a positive or negative column, but truly, there's so much more than just two columns. I've realized that experiences are often both positive and negative, which makes sense because life requires balance. From the positive, we learn gratitude for this gift we have been given, and from the negative, we learn lessons that may teach us important things we can use for the rest of our lives. People often say that in order to live a positive life, you need to focus on the positives, but I truly believe you're missing out on the real lessons by doing this and then often experience a positivity fog or become so positive it's almost toxic because it comes off as forced. The lesson does not typically lie in the positive. At least for me, the negative aspect of an experience is what holds the lesson. Then that lesson makes the experience more positive.

Before jumping to conclusions. I now ask myself three questions:

1. What lessons can be learned from this?
2. What can the positives be?
3. What negatives can I prepare for?

This stops me from categorizing things as solely positive or negative. They become a learning experience for me, and then things don't look too bleak or too good to be true anymore. Because that has been another lesson I had to learn the hard way. When something sounds too good to be true, it usually is. I could never list all the get-rich-quick schemes I tried to participate in. I swore I would be the best seller of cutlery, weight loss products, candles, and makeup at different points of my life. I couldn't wait to drive my new car and put the down payment on my new mansion. The only people who made money during those times in my life were those who got me started and the company that convinced me to sell their products.

As I started embracing my new attitude, I pushed those thoughts of dread out of my mind and stopped seeing things as piling up and burying me so deep I can't dig myself out and started seeing everything as an experience to learn from. I had often done small-scale versions of this in the past, but it was mostly for my business life. I needed to expand it to every facet of my life. That was hard to do at first. It was difficult to see the clear answer through the fog the depression was causing. It seems very simple, but it requires practice and patience to remember not to immediately fall apart when something perceived as bad happens.

A lot of people call this looking for the silver lining, and I was always told to look for the silver lining, but I was never told how to process my negative thoughts or feelings to find the elusive silver lining. It felt like giving a hungry baby a bowl of cereal and a spoon and telling them to eat. They were told the goal but not taught the process to achieve that goal. I had to learn it for myself, but I could have drawn that conclusion a lot sooner if I would have been offered a path to get there.

Even though I love journaling, I always wrote down

what was bothering me but rarely saw a path to a solution. I have started treating my problems like a business analysis. This way, I can really focus on the real problems and stay away from the surface problems. Once, prior to this, I was going through a range of emotions that were difficult to process. After looking it up, the emotions I was going through were the emotions of a typical grief process. Most don't relize that grief is not reserved for death. grief can be experienced in endless ways.

This is my grief process.

MY GREIF PROCESS

I knew that the grief process was typically something one goes through after experiencing death. However, I guess I was experiencing death. Pre-stroke me was dead. For the rest of my life, I will always be post-stroke Meetri'a. Even if I recover back to 100 percent and everything seems to settle back to how I was before, this experience will always be with me. I, for the rest of my life, I will have spent the better part of a year in a nursing home in recovery. I will always have not been living an independent life during 2023, and it doesn't matter if I like it or not—the pre-stroke me has absolutely passed and exists now only in memories. I feel thankful for that because I've seen what a stroke can cause. At least I still had some of me left. Every day,

I witness people trapped in the prison that is their post-stroke brain. Bodies that quit working and brains that convinced them they couldn't do anything to change their situation. At least I still had Meetri'a; I could have lost myself completely. Every day, I look around and originally saw despair, but slowly, it became fuel for my own recovery. More about that later. let's go through my grief process.

DENIAL

I spent months going through many different types of denial. I was in denial that I would have a new normal that I would approve of. I knew life would be different, but would the differences be something I could proudly live with? I was in denial that the stroke was not some sort of punishment or retaliation for something I had done. I was in denial that I would ever even recover. I assumed since my recovery could go wrong, it would. I had been told by several people that the ramifications of my stroke could lead to a completely different normal than before. The same way that the old me had died, a new me needed to be born, and I was denying that too. I was convinced that things would snap back, like a rubber band. I was denying myself the ability to recover smoothly.

I don't know why I was holding onto the old me; that old life was filled with misery and unaddressed trauma. Some caused by me, some caused by outside sources. That was something else I had learned through prior therapy. Accountability matters! I was allowed to be upset, but I was not allowed to blame others for things within my control. When the blame for all your problems gets placed on someone else, you truly have no control over your life. A lot of our lives are out of our control anyway; why give up more control? When you truly think about it, so much is within our control! We often fail to recognize it. Some submit to the notion that our lives are left up to chance. Others put their lives in "God's hands," and they give up control and let their lives fly on autopilot, and then they rationalize both the good and bad as "God's will." I don't want to knock people's beliefs or mock them, but how can you feel proud of your accomplishments when you can't claim the work you've done? How can you know your areas of improvement if you can't recognize where you're lacking? If there is a God and God gave us free will, isn't it arrogant to assume that God is constantly pulling the strings? I personally feel like it is. There were moments of light in my old life, not everything was terrible, but the darkness was overwhelming in many of those memories. Why not let go and start over? Maybe because starting over is scary. Maybe because it felt like a surrender. I didn't see starting over as a good thing for a while. I kept thinking if I let the old me die, that would be me giving up. I would be admitting defeat. I didn't want to give up because I was living in a place with people who had given up. Whatever their personal reasons for giving up is their business, but the results of giving up were visible all around me. A constant reminder of giving up was confined to a bed for the rest of their lives or sitting in wheelchairs unable to speak, constantly reliant on someone to move them around because they were incapable of being mobile on their own. One guy spent so much time fighting against his own recovery that he went from being able to get around on his own to losing the strength to get around on his own to being active in hospice and given six months to live. He wasn't a stroke patient, but he took no accountability and had no commitment to his recovery or himself. I watched him cry the day he got the news, and I felt awful for him, but all I could think about was how often he demanded others do things for him. He was capable of moving himself a little, but if there was a CNA around, he'd ask them to push him. Instead of trying to strengthen his muscles, he chose the easy way out. I would call that giving up. He blamed three different wheelchairs for his pain and kept making them get him new ones. No wheelchair was ever going to make his pain go away or help his recovery. I would never rub it in his face because I'm no one to make him feel like shit. But he would blame everyone else and everything else for him being in a difficult situation. It allowed him the freedom to give up fighting and put the blame on others. His power of denial was so strong that it was literally killing him. I was also in denial that things would have to change. There was no way to avoid change, and I couldn't see that initially. I didn't see it as releasing myself from the ties that bound me to my old life and allowing myself to start over. I also didn't know that I needed a rebirth. I didn't want to have the old me die. I liked er and I was scared to start over again. I had started over before, not quite to this extreme, but if that was hard, this was gonna be expert level. The fear of defeat and starting over was so scary, especially with new limitations. I was petrified, and the denial was like a permanent state I was in. At least it felt that way. Luckily, it wasn't permanent.

ANGER

My anger stage was a mixture of anger and resentment. Or more resentment that caused anger! I was angry that this happened to me, especially when I think I'm a good person. Was I a good person who was losing their way? Sure, but did that make me a bad person? According to many societal standards, yes, it did. Did I deserve to suffer a debilitating stroke? I didn't think so. That was something that I constantly thought about. Why did this happen to me? What did I do to deserve something like this? I spent a lot of my time while depressed, questioning what I had done that deserved a punishment like this. I had a conversation with my mom about this, and she explained that she had similar thoughts when she was diagnosed with stage four colon cancer. She had gone through a plethora of surgeries to help her, and every one of them shoved her mortality in her face. Every blood test and scan did the same. My mom, for the first time, opened up to me with more details about her journey and told me that she too questioned, "Why cancer?" and "Why me?" Death can come in many forms, but something like cancer doesn't just kill you. It tries erasing who you were by ruining you with disease and ailments that embarrass and humiliate you. You can lose your hair and waste away from chemo. You can lose control of bodily functions. My mother went through a surgery that took many of her organs and left her with a urostomy and a colostomy. She spent years acclimating to them.She felt like it was all punishment at first and realized later it wasn't punishment. It was a bad situation that appeared hopeless, but as she let go of the fear and focused on the fight, she found hope! She let go of the feeling of being punished and learned to fight for her recovery. With that fight, a lot of the anger melted away. I had yet to find my reason to fight. The anger was like a nice warm bath after playing in the snow–it was comfortable. It felt well deserved. I felt like after something like this stroke, I was allowed to be angry. My anger wasn't directed to the right person. My anger was directed toward the world because the world got to keep going while my world seemed to stop. I'd hear someone bitching about having to go to work, and it would piss me off. I would have given anything to be in a position to work again. My resentment was directed toward my friends and family because I felt like I was the only one negatively affected by my stroke. I felt like I had many close people in my life who turned their backs on me. I was displaced from my home and my normal routine, and there were times I felt like people were blaming me for what happened. I take full responsibility for the things I could have controlled, but my biological father had a stroke too, so it's my fault. But there were other things out of my control that contributed I felt like people were mad at me, so that was why they were not visiting or reaching out to me. I started feeling abandoned by people I had always been there for and family who I was told I could always count on. I think that part of the feelings was my stroke talking and part being upset, thinking that no one cared enough to save me from this travesty. I started feeling even more worthless. I kept thinking, Am I not worth saving?

I was living in a new world with new ailments, very few friends, and lots of loneliness to spare. I had family members who had the room and the money to help me, but they were not offering help. I wasn't even seeing them. This was a thought that lived in my head rent free, and every time I thought about it, it was like a green light for my depression to come in. In moments of clarity, I began to realize I wasn't thinking about the full situation or the limitations of some of those individuals. I was only thinking about myself. For some, there was no excuse other than I was not as important to them as they were to me. And that was very apparent once the fog had cleared. It was also important for me to have a solid support system. There were some core people who were always present, and to them, I am eternally grateful. And there were some others who were available to me, but they were not actively present. I am appreciative of them, and I also learned so much about them. There were others who would occasionally reach out and apologize for being absent during my time of need. In my opinion, they wanted me to give them a pass to feel better about themselves for not being a very good friend, especially when I would send out a help signal, and it would go unanswered. After, I was able to handle company again because for a while, all I wanted was company, a visitor, someone to talk to. I wanted to know what I was missing in the world. My FOMO was strong at this time. My loneliness often turned into anger. And my kindness turned into resentment. Eventually, it all turned to depression.

DEPRESSION

The depression stage hit me hard and fast and was present throughout all stages of my grief process. It literally hit within minutes of me getting to the hospital. I can recall my depression not giving away until around August. My birthday ironically was the thing that started the unraveling process to the tangled web that was my depression.

Since the moment I was admitted to each hospital and then the nursing home, I wanted to know when I could leave. I wanted a discharge date to count down to. I always, in some way, thought that with a discharge date, my recovery would go much faster. I wanted nothing more than to go home. I learned the hard way that the brain chooses its own speed of recovery. Every day spent away from the life I had known and grown accustomed to felt like a personal failure. Each failure was another foot deeper into the hole of depression I had been trying to dig myself out of. It often felt like a hopeless and endless task. I had to find a way to be happy but being happy in a nursing home felt like I was admitting defeat. It felt like all the crying and the phone calls spent complaining were all for naught.

When I realized that I was a long way away from a discharge date, I promised myself that I would not spend my birthday in a nursing home. It just didn't seem appropriate for a thirty-seven-year-old. As my birthday approached, I kept hoping for a break. My current mode of transportation was a motorized wheelchair; it was donated to me by my grandmother. Even though she and I haven't had a relationship in years, she was kind enough to give me the motorized chair that a disabled man that was living with her for a while owned and left behind when he passed from COVID. It was very heavy and very difficult to transport. Unfortunately, I also no longer had money coming in, so I was broke and wasn't really able to be transported without my chair for the most part. I had not yet tested my capabilities. I didn't know what I was capable of or where my limitations were. I had a resident come to my door early on in my stay at the nursing home. He wanted to introduce himself to me and make sure I was okay. He noticed I had stuck to my room for a long time and understood that this place caused depression when you entered it. I don't know if it was the feeling of the impending end or if it was the screams of pain, the piercing sounds of the call lights, or simply the alone time we had to sit and think, but it's no wonder that depression spread like the plague through this place. In fact, I was severely disappointed that there was no focus on mental health in a place where dementia lived in every other room. A therapist walking around would have been ideal. After checking on me, he and I became fast friends. He taught me how to play dominoes and often stopped by my room for conversation. He honestly was one of the first men in my life to be present and not expect something from me other than friendship. Between him and a few other close people, my birthday was celebrated with some dinner brought in to me, some cupcakes, some presents, and some games of dominoes. My birthday turned out not to be as sad as I expected, and I started feeling some love while stuck in this depressing place. It was promising that I felt good on a day I was sure would cause me pain.

My depression didn't lift completely until a little later though. Only then was I able to start accepting and coming to terms with my new life. The depression would still come and go randomly but nothing as severe as what hit me initially. It would suddenly hit me like a gust of wind. It would blow away my good mood and my feelings of "okay-ness," and just as the wind cools your skin while you are sunbathing at the beach, the depression and darkness would cool the warmth of the moments of light. Those moments of happiness took a lot of weight off my heart and my shoulders. When depression would hit me, the weight would return, and I would be in constant pain until my depression would lift. I could not and did not want to explain what was hurting. It was often inexplicable; I couldn't target the source of pain because it wasn't physical. Giving me a painkiller was not going to work. My anguish was not curable with a pill. It was mental pain. It was an emotional hurt. I was told to go outside or go eat with the other residents in the din -

ing room or do some activities with people. It was so hard to socialize. Socializing felt like submitting to this place. I could understand greta garbo when she said, "I want to be alone."

The problem was, being left alone allowed me time to think. I'm a solution-oriented person so thinking brought up many other questions, which dug me deeper in that pit of depression because with questions, I kept finding more problems or obstacles that needed more solutions. Which led to more thinking, which led to more questions. It was a cycle of perpetual depression. And getting it to go away seemed impossible.

BARGAINING

I started trying to get rid of the depression using bargaining talk. looking back, this is the funniest time of my recovery.

I would lay in bed constantly for the first few months, spending hours bargaining with anyone who would listen to me. I remember devoting myself to any being of power that would help me. I even offered my soul to Satan at one point. I didn't care who helped me; I only cared that I was reset, even back to somewhat normal. I offered to devote my life to helping people if I got function back in my arm and leg. I remember even telling people so that I could hold myself accountable. I remember telling people that if I got back my walking and had full control of my arm and hand, I would go into nursing or CNA work.

Looking back on it, I can only laugh because I would bargain with anyone and everyone. I couldn't see that I was bargaining with the wrong people. No God came through for me, no Devil came through for me, no family saved me, no one came through for Meetri'a, except Meetri'a. I should have spent those hours bargaining with myself. Motivating myself to continue. Convincing myself that my hard work panned out before. My right side is essentially fully healed and back to normal function. It gives me hope that with time and effort, my left side could heal the same or close to the same. Why didn't I focus on that from the beginning? I believe it's because a depressed brain can't see the same clear path as a non-depressed one. I was dealing with a depressed brain after a stroke; the path was filled with obstacles like a road under construction in Michigan in June. I couldn't see that I was my own best advocate and my own confidence booster. I motivated myself to keep moving forward. Others cheered me on, but the majority of the faith in me that I felt came from me. The bargaining didn't last long, maybe because I was on the verge of a breakthrough or maybe because I was convinced that I would be ignored and life would shit on me again and hang me out to dry. In my past life, when I usually prayed for something to happen to make my life a little better, it wouldn't happen. Murphy's law, right? It was like life's little joke on me. I gave up on bargaining. No amount of crystals, encouragement, or openness to the powers mattered. I started seeing that I had the power all along. It was a ruby slipper realization. This was when everything changed for the better.

ACCEPTANCE

The idea of accepting my current situation was a large and a jagged pill to swallow, but I figured out how to accept what was happening to me. The acceptance to me was less about accepting the current situation and more about understanding my situation. So I spent a lot of time exploring stroke information and exercises to help regain my movements like I did after my first stroke.

As I began understanding my condition, I started understanding more about what it would take to go home, even though I had no physical home anymore. Home for me was just a place where I could feel comfortable and independent, being around friends who weren't catering to me. At the time, it could have been very difficult. When I'd question why I was still sitting in a nursing home and why I wasn't being "rescued," I would breathe, and I'd rationalize that this really was the best place for me at the time. I wouldn't have the kind of assistance I had here if I was home or if I was in a new home with friends or family. I started understanding that other people have lives and families of their own to take care of, and it wasn't fair to them for me to be dropped off at their doorstep. It was difficult to come to that realization when I was so down in the dumps. It was difficult to see through the fog; it just felt like abandonment and my depressed brain cosigned that notion. In fact, it typically doubled down on that notion until I was inconsolable. With moments that the fog of depression lifted came me, trying to remember I was in the process of accepting my new self. It helped me start getting through this recovery a little easier. Accepting that this stroke happened and that there was no going back in time; no matter how many whiskey bottles I polished off was difficult to accept. It's difficult when you come to terms with the fact that time travel really is only in movies.

After I began the acceptance stage, things seemed better. It took accepting this recovery as a new start. I seemed to wake up lighter. I was happier. I realized that being happy here was not defeat. The only defeat I was facing was me defeating myself and trying to embrace my sadness. I felt so dumb for stopping my own happiness for so long when I realized that's what I had been doing. I learned to be happy here and not let my broken expectations of others bring me down. I finally accepted the death of the old me. I accepted that happiness in a place where I was miserable was not a defeat. I felt my life turning around. I felt that I had found a way to get through this. I was feeling really good about everything, and then I was tested by the universe. I felt my strength returning and, with it, my confidence.

My confidence outweighed my abilities, and I decided I could go to the toilet myself that day. I had a very steady walk to the bathroom, and I was able to get my pants and underwear off without losing my balance. I sat down with purpose and intent, something I had been working on with therapy. When I finished, I leaned forward to wipe, and the strength and balance required to do that kind of leaning had not yet been restored. Because my ambition had gotten the better of me, I fell off the toilet face-first. As I went crashing to the floor, I had enough time to try catching myself, which actually bruised the wrist of my good hand. I bloodied my chin from smashing my face into the porcelain bathtub that just took up space in my bathroom. I feared I had set myself back, but luckily, I had only bruised my wrist, my chin, and my ego. I didn't have the strength or ability to get off the floor, but I was able to reach the emergency call light in the bathroom.

Approximately five minutes later, I shocked the aide who entered my room when I greeted her from the bathroom floor. Looking back on it, it was a funny situation. I had to be dragged out of my bathroom on a sheet, into the middle of my bedroom floor with no bottoms. I had to roll over both directions while half naked to get a sling under me. They then brought a Hoyer Lift, which I hadn't been in for months. They lifted me off the floor into my bed and cleaned me up. I cried from embarrassment and regret from thinking I could do normal things again.

As I felt the negative thoughts seeping in and flooding my brain, I remembered that while the final destination was not planned this way, I was still successful. I didn't plan on falling, but I did walk to the bathroom, I did get my clothes off, and I did sit down without plopping down! There were many high- lights to this journey. Between those highlights and remembering where I started and where I was now definitely contributed to me reaching the acceptance stage of my grieving process. After realizing that I was truly making progress, I realized I was not going to remain at the starting line forever; there was a path I was going down. Maybe I was going slow, but we were always told that slow and steady can win the race. Then I realized there was a recovery possible. It may not lead to my old normal, but it definitely would lead to my new normal. And that was a path once clouded with the fog of depression and fear. It was suddenly a path that was clear as day now, and the depression has been replaced by hope and motivation; the fear has been replaced with optimism.

I was once told by a very close friend that I was allowed to go to those places. The places where I feel bad for myself and I get depressed and I want to give up, I can go there, but I can't stay–I'm allowed to have my feelings, and I'm allowed to have irrational thoughts, I'm allowed to be mad at the world, but I need to remember that I am just driving through. I'm allowed to go there, By accepting my new normal and my new process of approaching situations, I feel my future has new life lessons and purposes beyond what I could imagine. At least I hope so. We never know what the future holds, do we? It's always such a mystery. For instance, as a young gay boy, I felt like the black sheep of my family. I had a gay step-uncle, and I always heard close family talking shit about him. Because of what was always said behind his back, I tried to be nothing like him. Looking back, I find it funny that I turned out very similar to him. I tried to avoid being looked at differently, but the universe saw that in my future.

That wasn't the only experience that scared me from being who I was. As a young child and in my early teens, I would be with my grandmother a lot. She considers herself a good Christian. She also worked as a pharmacy technician, so as a younger child, I assumed that meant she was very knowledgeable in the medical world. I was with her one day, and I asked what she knew about AIDS. I had heard about it as early as my elementary health class. She told me that she knew a lot about it. So feeling safe, I asked her how AIDS happened to people who didn't have it. I followed it up with a scenario—I asked if my uncle was at risk. I had also been told previously that HIV and AIDS were prominent in the gay community. She told me that the product of anal sex was AIDS. I was terrified to be who I felt I was inside, and I had already had my first sexual experiences. Was I going to be made fun of by my own family and possibly die from something so deadly? I had always felt shame for being who I was. I felt like I had disappointed them because I was attracted to guys. Luckily, that shame didn't faze, me and I remained me.

BEFORE AND AFTER ACCEPTANCE

I met my chosen family at a drag show. In my twenties, I had been dabbling in drag but really wanted to dive deeper. Being in drag unlocked a person that was pressured to stay hidden for so long. Drag helped me find my real personality. I also unlocked the confidence to be myself, Even in a world that told me I was wrong. Through a lesson in how to do drag makeup, I met a family that was gay like I thought I was, and they accepted me as I was. I was fine as I was. My drag mother was like another mother to me. She—he prefers he/him pronouns but doesn't mind she/her as a mother figure—was supportive and nurturing. Her husband was like the first father figure in my life who actually acted like a father to me. He was protective and proud of his children. They were there for their drag children. Being with them just felt like how home should feel. As some families do, we had a pretty big falling out. I assumed I had burned that bridge. A mutual friend of ours and also chosen family to me, reconnected us again, and after some conversations and apologies, we were on better terms. Our friend is also a drag queen but has an old soul and loves to remind us of where we were as an LGBTQ+ community and where we are now and how far we've come. Very much like a grandmother. When this stroke hit me, some of my biological family was there to cheer me on in my recovery, but my chosen family was with me at least once a week. I didn't expect them to stick it out with me when my recovery seemed to take a while. When others fell off, my chosen family was still present. Between them and some others who I have known for years, I call them my sisters. My chosen family stood beside me both figuratively and literally, holding my hand and watching me work what I could to get better. I was fighting for my recovery. I was sure they would disappear like everyone else had, but they didn't. I will forever be grateful to my chosen family for being such an integral part of my recovery.

That wasn't my first major fall in my recovery or my first major breakthrough. About a month into my stay, I was deep in a fog. I watched the snow falling outside my window, and it mockingly danced in the air to the ground as if to say, "Ha ha, I'm outside having fun, and you have to lay in bed!" I would have killed to step outside in my winter boots and my new winter coat I bought. It was a peacoat that had a tie around the waist and flared at the bottom It was lined with a leopard-printed satin, and it fit like a glove. When I tried it on, it was like it was made for me. I would have given anything to wear that coat and feel the cold winter air on my face and maybe even catch a snowflake on my tongue. The nostalgia of that thought alone gave my FOMO (the fear of missing out) more power. I had no idea what the universe had in store for me that winter. I was so focused on what I could have been missing out on that I couldn't see what was happening was the plan. I was lost in thought about what I was missing. Before my stroke, I was being interviewed for a new property management job with a salary of $85,000 a year and free housing. It required a move, which I always looked forward to. I felt I was missing out on a new place, new experiences, and who knew what else. I was feeling sorry for myself as I drifted off to sleep. I had been complaining that my bed felt short, and I felt cramped in my bed. Remember, I previously had a California king bed. I'm also six feet four and over 350 pounds. I moved my good leg and, with it, my left leg by hooking the left leg with my right foot. If you just made a joke about me being a hooker, congrats, we are now friends. My left leg was not moving at the time. The dead weight of my left leg pulled my body down, and I rolled right off the bed. On the way down, I had enough time to grab the emergency call light and push a nightstand out of the way before hitting my head against it. It was almost like in slow motion. On the way down, I remember yelling out, "Motherfucker!" and then hitting the ground. Nothing was bruised or broken, just my ego. This was months before the second fall off the toilet, so this was a new kind of embarrassment I was experiencing. like I said, I had enough awareness of the situation to snatch the call light before I left the bed. I tried getting up on my own, but I wasn't able to position my feet well enough to get the leverage when I pushed against the floor. I was immediately brought back to the reality that I was in a very helpless situation. I hit my call light and waited for help. I laid on the cold hard floor for at least five minutes before yelling out, "Help!" hoping someone would hear me. I had found in my short time in the nursing home that there was a natural disstain of the heavier patients, like me. The heavy patients required additional equipment and extra work, so I often found my room being avoided because if I had to use the commode, my aide would have to sling me up on the sit-to-stand machine, and it required more work. I truly hated having to hit my light for anything because everything felt like an inconvenience. I read vibes pretty well, and I always felt like I was interrupting their day.

I lay on the floor, waiting for help, and I had a great view of the crack under the door. I watched people walk by my room, ignoring my room light flashing in the hallway, not knowing I lay helpless on the floor. Luckily, not with a life-threatening injury. I screamed, "Help!" as loud as I could. My screams went unanswered, and as dramatic as it sounds, I felt like I was living my own horror movie. My own body had betrayed me, and like a thief in the night, the stroke stole my ability to use half of my body. It was a theft that hurt worse than being stabbed. I've never been stabbed, but I assume it's not a pleasant feeling. The villain of this movie wasn't a hockey mask-wearing, machete-wielding maniac; it was invisible and almost supernatural. The big twist was that my body was the victim and my brain was the villian. There was no hiding or running to safety. It was terrifying. I felt rendered helpless, and there was no retribution that could make me feel like justice had been served. I lay on the floor watching people walk by with little effort. What an embarrassing thing to be envious of—walking—it was for me anyway. My heart goes out to those who deal with that kind of envy. I can say that I truly understand your feelings. The cold floor sent chills through my body, and nothing could warm me at that moment. I felt cold, alone, and trapped. Trapped in a body that didn't work right. Trapped in a nursing home where no one could see me. Then I finally heard a voice outside the door and saw footsteps moving toward my room. I remember thinking, Someone finally wants to help me?

The CNA walked in and looked down at the floor and rolled her eyes. It was then that I realized she wasn't there to help me, but she was there to turn off my call light. Then she snarkily spat out, "Really?" as if to say, "You did this on purpose, didn't you?" Pissed off and offended were gross understatements of my feelings. If I had the power of pyrokinesis, I would have set her on fire and watched her burn. And as my grandmother once said, I wouldn't piss up her ass if her guts were on fire. I had a special kind of hate for that woman. I try to see good in everybody, and I don't like the word hate. I try to show everyone love and kindness.

They finally had gotten me up and back in bed, and I was able to relax. I continued to watch the snow fall gently from the sky and collect on the ground as I continued feeling bad for myself. In my head,, I went to a place where I was fine, and I was walking in Bronson Park in downtown Kalamazoo. I was looking at all the lights while walking under the giant candy canes that lined the sidewalk. I was enjoying a winter wonderland, and I had an ear full of Christmas music. I was not nursing a bruised ego after a little accident while feeling bad for myself.

It wasn't until the next morning that I had a breakthrough with my recovery. I will never know if it was the fall or all the work in physical therapy that I had been putting in or a mix of both. That next morning, I was able to move my leg again! It was an amazing breakthrough. It was still weak, and I had to build up the strength in it, but it made me feel enlightened for a while. The depression fog lifted, and the outlook was far less bleak. I began thinking that with this newfound movement, it was likely other things could recover too. It was another milestone that was worth holding onto in those times of darkness.

But as happy as I was, I couldn't let go of how the aide acted toward me. I have been in customer service for over twenty years. I knew how to treat people with dignity and how to show them that they are important.

I was also a property manager for six years and ran teams as small as two and as large as fifteen. I spent a long time observing people and analyzing behaviors, and that was only as a woman who was only working for the paycheck. I completely understand that money is the biggest motivation for working; you need money for bills and extracurriculars. But I think if you're working in a job that could impact the well-being of others exponentially, you should have some kind of passion for that work. Shouldn't you? I mean, no one sits in thought dreaming of a career where you clean up bodily fluids and poop and then are later abused by those same people you're cleaning up after. But if you choose that career, there should be more of a reward than just the money.

I spent a lot of time thinking about what was happening to me, and I decided to not let creative thoughts go to waste. So I started working on many creative things. Before my stroke, I loved sewing and crafting. I especially loved stoning things. It's like bedazzling but with more precision, with much higher quality stones, and by hand. I also love writing. I have l oved writing since high school. luckily, both things really only require one hand to do. They're easier with two hands but one will do. I had an iPhone and an iPad with me during my recovery, so I started several manu- scripts while in my new temporary home. I've always been a very creative person, so nothing was gonna stop me. I couldn't paint with my hands, but I could often paint with my mind. luckily, this brain injury damaged my physical body, but I was still pretty good mentally. The stories and worlds I could create in my head always felt like a blockbuster movie in my head but putting pen to paper was always a struggle, so I've tried for years to stumble through it and find a method that works for me. After I started acclimating to the new community of people I was surrounded by, I thought of a book to honor the lives of some of the residents that lived here. I sat down and started writing about some of the people who are going to end their lives here and how in their final days, they had no visitors and, for some, no one even checked up on them. They only saw or talked to nurses giving them medication or the CNAs that were offering other care if they could even talk. I feel like a lot of humans want nothing more than to be remembered. They may or may not fear death but being forgotten in this gigantically small world is a fate worse than death for some. I was going to call it The Forgotten because most of them didn't have to die to be forgotten; they just had to experience a huge medical event and then poof! They wound up in this waiting room, waiting for the end. It broke my heart to think that these people lived lives and likely had friends and family and experi-ences who could inspire other people, and in their end stage of life, they are left only with their memories of what used to be. Some were not even fortunate enough to have those. It was also sad to think that I could be in the same position at the end of my life. It was a reasonable thought because I had no children I would leave behind. I had no husband. It's a real possibility that I could be in the same position. I chose to immortalize these people and tell as much of their story as I could because they also have been part of my motivation to stay alive and focus on my recovery. If they could stay alive and continue on with life in this place, why couldn't I? I was grateful to many of these people for the motivation they unknowingly provided me. That project sits on the shelf until I can work out some of the logistics.

After my idea for The Forgotten got held up, I decided to write about how my entire life I've lived like I was surviving. In my life, I've experienced hardships that always felt like I was being tested. Some worse than others, some my fault, others beyond my control. And miraculously, I've always survived. But for a while, I lived like I was always anticipating the next blow. While writing that manuscript, I decided it was a message that could be improved upon. A lot of the stories of my survival made it into this book, but the message was going to be that it's okay to survive through life and often it will make you stronger. It's true, but we shouldn't waste our lives waiting for the house of cards to collapse. We should attempt to live this life and not just survive through it.

When I started second-guessing the message of that book, I chose to take a new perspective of the same idea and started writing a book called Beautiful and Cruel. It was about my life experiences and how this world is beautiful and filled with wonderful gifts but also how this life is cruel as fuck! From the moment we peak adulthood, we immediately begin to age, wither, and eventually die. It's guaranteed for everyone. We are given this amazing gift of life only to be guaranteed it will be taken from us. So many talk about winning life, but ultimately, no one truly wins. Every human lives to face the same final destination. I wrote about how the perfect example of life is a rose–it is beautiful when fully bloomed, and as beautiful as it is, it has to be handled with care or you will be stabbed by the thorns. The point of this beautiful and cruel existence is to enjoy the beauty and do your best to avoid the thorns. I love this message, but while writing about the beautiful cruelty of life, I started talking about how balance is also guaranteed through life. Understanding the balance of life is vital for happiness. I had spent thirty-six years of my life believing that I was destined for the negative column of the world and there was no way to change it. Every time something good happened, something bad always seemed to be on its heels. Maybe it seemed like that because I was manifesting negativity into my life. I was putting positive out there into the universe, hoping my karma bank was building up, but while I was putting positivity out, living like a survivor was automatically expecting the negative. Expecting the negative was manifesting it into my life. Understanding that there is balance in life means understanding that there can be positive and negative experiences and understanding that there can be negativity in the positive experiences and there can be positivity in the negative experiences. Understanding that helped me find happiness during the most tragic time of my life.

As I encountered terrible CNAs, I also encountered some CNAs who did actually care. A great example was an aide who I will never forget, and I hope I have a relationship with her outside of this place. She was a very kind woman of color. She and I had an immediate connection. She was always in good spirits and work was never an aggravating chore. She would spread good energy around the building. There was a patient here whose health was fading quickly. The aide had a such a connection with her that as the patient was actively passing away, the aide had a feeling that something was wrong. She rushed to the patient's bedside and held her hand while she passed. The patient asked if they were still friends and apologized for not being able to stay longer. The aide accepted the apology and told her the apology was not necessary, and if she felt like it was time to go, she could go. She got to hold the hand of a friend as she passed on, and according to her, she saw her mother coming for her. When I was told about that experience, I cried. I can only hope for the same. We all die alone but having someone there to show you love as you pass sounds ideal. I can only imagine that is the best feeling. leaving this world knowing you were cared about has to be much better than dying scared and alone. That aide is somebody who does healthcare work because she cares. The aide who came into my room and saw me on the floor and only saw more work definitely needs to find a new career. I know for a fact she got a new job because she was not seen again after that day. If you're that CNA and you're reading this, understand that empathy goes a long way, and I truly hope you have the life you deserve. After that fall, I kept trying to recover as much as I could. My insurance had warned that it was about to run out. I had no choice but to learn as much as I could because I'm used to having control, and I learned early to ask questions to get things done. Very rarely was information voluntarily given out; I often had to go through a barrage of questions to get the answer I was looking for. At the hospitals things seemed to be far more organized. That was to be expected, but when I arrived at the nursing home, I was told absolutely nothing. I wasn't told how meals worked. I wasn't told about activities. I wasn't told about showers. I didn't expect everything to be the same, but I did expect to still feel somewhat human. I showered every day at home. I was getting bed baths every day at the hospitals. I was only required two showers a week at the nursing home because that was the "minimum standard of care." I was only required to receive the minimum standard of care for the maximum cost. You'd think a place charging $221 a day could afford to do a little more than the minimum standard. It was appalling that most of these people were only an occupied bed to the top line. You can tell because simple things were overlooked almost diligently. like why was a patient's glasses broken for over five months when the nursing home organized the mobile optometrist? That is such a long time to sit with blurry vision. I watched another woman begging to get off her feeding tube. They would never try to rehabilitate her. I heard her beg for food, and she just wanted to taste real food again. There was never an effort to help her get better. It took effort to ignore some of their cries for help. There were some people that the goal was just to keep them alive. As long as they were alive, the money kept rolling in for them occupying a bed. Others were in for rehabilitation, but you'd never know it unless they were seen with therapy. When they were with other staff, they were treated like a nursing home patient that they tried to keep alive, not someone they could rehabilitate. These are my observations and my personal opinions.

But part of my job at one point was to find the disconnects in the daily operations of a business and fix them. I can spot where systems are lacking minutes after walking into an establishment. I say it is definitely a gift and a curse. It certainly caused me some moments of contention while I was here. But those moments were more motivation to keep getting better. I've never had a problem speaking up when something is not correct. There was always an excuse to get them out of doing anything more than the minimum standard even if it was far more humane When I confronted the dietary manager, I quickly figured out why the kitchen staff lacked accountability. The one in charge also lacked accountability. There was an excuse for everything brought up to him. I soon found that with other department leads also. When you don't take accountability for your shortfalls, how do you expect your department to run efficiently? You can't. It was soon apparent that the shit rolled downhill here. I found that head leadership not only lacked experience but also ambition to do right by the residents. He only cared about his appearance; he never cared about the residents. He had to be dressed the nicest and had to wear the loudest cologne so you'd know he was here, but he let his department leads run the show so no standards were ever put in place. When they wanted something, it was usually approved because when you tell the people running the show no, they stop working as hard, and it leaves you with more to do. They also lacked procedure standards. I watched a man start his job and walk out days later because everything was a confusing mess. I offered to help in any way I could because I wanted to feel needed and useful again. I also had no money anymore. Having low or no funds always puts me ina depressed state. I figured the place dealing with my limitations would be open-minded enough to accept and accommodate my limitations in a work scenario. The only job offer I got from them was to be paid in pop or candy to help out. I was worth having on the staff to work, but I wasn't worth being paid real money.

I knew my worth. I obviously declined that offer. I may have a few physical ailments, but I'm worth more than pop or candy. Fixing this place would require a lot of work and would need to start with people opening their eyes. Neither of the two were gonna happen anytime soon, so I gave up on trying to fix anything from the inside. I was still resident of this place, and I had a voice. I decided to start taking the actions I could take. I've always tried to remember to only worry about the things I can control, and I had a whole system I could control from where I sat. It was almost more powerful than being an employee because residents had a lot of power here. The question was whether or not they had the facilities to comprehend their abilities and how to utilize them. luckily for me and unfortunately for the nursing home, I was fully aware and cognizant of my rights and abilities. So I controlled what I could to make my life easier while living there. The one thing I will say that was positive about this period of my stay was that the constant fighting with this place somewhat gave me purpose. I didn't go out of my way to find fights, but when I came across them, I started working on changing things. Then I finally started coming out of my room because when I was finally able to start being mobile, I still didn't leave my room. When I did start getting out, I would sit next to the nurse's station. I had seen many other people sit there, and there was usually someone there to talk to. That was always nice because in here, mental health was not a priority. If you had dementia, it was important to them, but you had to tell people you were depressed for them to recognize a change in your mood or behavior. At least having someone around to shoot the shit with was better than sitting in my bed, roaming around my head all day, thinking about what used to be. As I sat there, people wouldn't think twice about discussing someone's health information. I tried to not listen, but as I mentioned before, my job required a strong ability to observe. That meant using all five senses, especially the ability to listen to my surroundings and what was happening around me. I'd try not to listen, but my brain would automatically process information it was hearing.

One day, I literally got shooed away from my normal spot, hand motions and all. This didn't sit right with me. Obviously me being around the nurse's station had gotten around because people started saying things to me like, "You know too much" or "You don't work here!" I found it funny because through the simple task of paying attention, I knew when people had appointments, who was on the schedule to work, what rooms people were in, and more importantly when people needed help. This pissed people off because I would tend to know more about this place than they did. Some joked about it and said, "You know everything that's going on." The ones who got mad were the ones that would tell me, "You don't work here" or "You know too much." It was them trying to deter me from coming up there. It didn't deter me from shit; I felt so good being able to still recognize things like that in that way. It helped me believe I could still be a high value manager, and I could still offer those same skills I had before. They thought I was being nosy, but I was rehabilitating! A fact I could never get through to these people. They knew I wasn't elderly, and they could see I was getting better all the time, but it never clicked that I was rehabilitating. But I suppose that requires attention to detail and common sense. So I had been shooed away, and I was immediately upset that I was treated like a child and told to shoo instead of being asked like an adult. Had she said, "Can you please give the social worker a moment to talk with this family in private?"I would have been far more receptive, and I would have given them some space. After she walked away, I went up to the administrator and expressed my issue with what happened. To which he responded by telling me that I was in the wrong and shouldn't be stationed in that spot."Why was I never told that?" I asked, feeling that this was going to get heated. "Well, this is the nurse's station. We get phone calls about private matters and residents shouldn't be sitting up here," he said, trying to prove a point. "So if residents shouldn't be up here, why are other residents around the nurse's station when they are wheeled out here?" I clapped back, pointing to three other residents within earshot of the same station residents shouldn't be around. "Well, they won't understand the conversation they overhear," he said this with a straight face, thinking that he has checked me. "So because I am capable of understanding the conversation, I am not allowed to be in a residential area, but since they may not understand the conversation, they can be wherever? That sounds like bullshit to me. If that private conversation is so important, take it somewhere private. I'm not the one violating HIPAA by being in earshot of a private conversation. You are in violation of HIPAA by having that conversation within earshot of me," I explained while delivering a death blow to the argument. From that moment on, when a private conversation started in front of me, someone would inevitably ask them to take it off the floor. Some would even nod their head toward me, indicating, "look who's around." I loved this because obviously there was a conversation about this issue, and what should have been a policy already was now being enforced. I created that change! I had proven my theory that residents did have power in there. Had management been doing their job, they wouldn't have needed me to intervene through the back door, but I was happy to play them like I used to play with my action figures. Maybe it's manipulative, but I wouldn't want someone overhearing personal medical information about me. So I chose to take action, and it worked out in everyone's favor. The point is I started feeling that I hadn't lost my touch! This stroke took a lot from me, but I was still able to identify a problem and find a solution and a path to achieve that solution. I started feeling a little more normal. I was still smart and sassy and still had a solution-oriented way of thinking. It felt like the old me hadn't fully died. There were still pieces of the old me in myself. That felt incredibly positive to me. Then I could realize that my rebirth had to happen for me to truly be healed and happy. I know the cliché of a phoenix rising from the ashes is so over-used and cringe for many, but that is the best example I can give after coming to terms with the new me. It was time to be renewed. I feel like the reset button on my life was hit. I can't replay all the levels over, but I can do so many things over. It's the perfect time for a career and a lifestyle change. It's the perfect time to get rid of some vices and regrow the adult me. There's no perfect time for a devastating life event, but maybe for me there was. As I claimed my truth as a woman named Meetri'a, maybe it was also the push I needed to find my purpose in life. Like anyone in this world, I feel I searched for a purpose for so long it always felt like the answer was there, but I could never identify it..

I know I've always felt happiest while creating. I have

been writing for years. Whether it was my journal to reflect on my day or in a notebook, wanting to develop a new hit TV show. Never seriously but always with a sprinkle of hope that I would eventually create something that would help people. Most creative minds want their work to inspire someone. And that's all I want to do. When this stroke hit me the one thing I've heard at least one hundred times was that I was "way too young to have a stroke." I always thought to myself, What is the right age for a stroke? There isn't one. After my stroke, I watched over a dozen stories of others having a stroke. And they were all different ages and different genders, and they were all in different occupations. There was no common thread of cause. The stories I saw never discussed the part of the journey that could really mess you up—the mental roller coaster a major life event can put you on. I wanted to tell my story to let others know they are not alone, even when you feel completely alone. That was very important to me because I was "too young to have a stroke," so I was not fully prepared for the implications of a large medical event. The hospital, the testing, the changes were all foreign. While I was unprepared, so was my support system; we all had to learn and adjust. But whoever is prepared for a medical event? If we knew things like this were going to happen, we might actually change our behaviors to avoid it. There's usually a warning, but we tend to feel invincible until we find out we are not. I had definitely had my ideas of invincibility shattered. Facing your mortality is very stressful and extremely trying. It is also filled with emotions you've never felt and others you've never wanted to feel again. All I wanted was to go back to the old me, but the old me was killing me. Looking back, I can say that with confidence. I can always say that the journey I was able to go on from this stroke was so beneficial for me. It was a road under construction at first. But eventually, we got through the rough parts and got to the smooth road. But that's life, isn't it? Balancing out the rough road with the smooth road. Balancing out the darkness with beams of light. Balancing out the light with shade. Balance may not come in the form that we want it, but my eyes were opened to accepting what I need even if I don't want it. A lot of life is like walking a tightrope and balance is the key. Maybe people have known this for a long time, but it has taken me thirty-seven years to really embrace it. It's always been in front of me, but my depression often blinded me. It's hard to come to terms with something when you're the one who pulled the wool over your own eyes. Sometimes the hardest part is admitting you are causing your own pain. That requires accountability. In 2016, I had my first DUI while living in Michigan. By 2019, I had been promoted in my career and moved to Pennsylvania. In 2019, I got pulled over again and received my second DUI. During my first DUI, I vividly remember blaming everyone else for my DUI. I blamed the police for not having anything better to do. I blamed the bartenders for over-serving me. I blamed the girls that bought me shots all night. I blamed one of my friends for not coming out that night, who could have driven me. I blamed my stepfather for fucking me up enough that I turned to drinking to cope. I blamed everyone and everything that sounded at all reasonable. During my second DUI, I was mandated to alcohol counseling, and I learned that I was responsible for my own actions. I was the one who went to the bar that night. I was the one who drank the shots that were bought for me. I was the one who put the key in the ignition. I was the one who was driving intoxicated. My childhood trauma was outside of my control, and it was a choice by another human, but it was my choice to cope by numbing the pain with alcohol. When I faced the truth, I was able to see that I was in charge of all those actions.

I was once again hurting myself. I started always recognizing that I was responsible for my actions. I can't control others or their actions, but I can control how I handle the actions of others or the lack of actions by others. It was important to remember this during my medical recovery when others would disappoint me. I often leaned on the fact that I have always learned to adjust to new environments, situations, and people when it mattered. But accepting any form of what was happening with me subconsciously meant defeat. No one likes the idea of surrendering. I included. But defeat wasn't always present in the form of defeat. Defeat comes in many forms. Like writer's block, for instance.

I was always able to get a good idea down on paper, but the meat of the story always seemed difficult. This stroke caused me to be in the hospital, which caused me to lose everything. My apartment complex evicted me, rendering me essentially homeless. I had a roof over my head but not anything I could call my own. When the eviction was processed, they threw away most of my personal belongings. My car went up for repossession. My income stopped almost immediately. I lost friendships I thought were timeless and so much more. This started in winter. I watched the snow fall, collect on the ground, and begin to melt as the temperatures were on the rise. I watched spring come and breathe renewed life into the outside world. I watched summer enter and heat things up. I watched fall cool things down, and I watched the leaves change, and my favorite season sat waiting for me. I used to feel like the world was moving on without me, but the truth is my world didn't stop—I was in a cocoon, transforming. As I look back on everything that happened, I thought I was a lost cause. I wasn't a lost cause; I was definitely lost, but I was able to come to terms with trauma that had been affecting me for a long time. I even think the way through the pain and suffering caused by this finally helped realize my dream of being a writer. I thought my story could inspire people, and that's all I've ever wanted to do. I hope that if nothing else, one of the scenarios I've talked about has made you realize that you can get through whatever you're going through. You don't have to be going through a medical emergency; you could be dealing with a vile stepparent or a strange new environment. Maybe you're experiencing grief due to a significant loss. Perhaps you are in the middle of the new you being born. The negative isn't always bad and the positive isn't always good. There is a balance to this thing called life and may the universe put only what we can handle in our path. I was convinced that this time I was in a situation that I wasn't strong enough to navigate. I learned I definitely was. While defeat comes in many forms, so does recovery! I was able to recover from so many issues during what seemed like the worst time of my life. I was also able to take away some great things from this.

TAKEAWAYS

No matter what anyone says, the one person who won't let you down is you! Balance is okay and inevitable. People choosing to treat you poorly is not the universe teaching you a lesson; it's a choice made by someone with bad intentions. You are your own best advocate. Half of your body may be on hiatus, and you can't type ninety words a minute anymore, but you can still write a book. Recovering from anything requires you to put the work in. It's okay to drive through the bad times, but don't stay there. You can get out. It's okay to have and process emotions. Be you and be happy. It's okay to reinvent yourself; there are no rules for it. Lastly, but not leastly, you are not alone!

I also learned to humble myself and learn to care about my mortality. When this happened, I didn't care about my health. I can confidently say it's now under control. My blood sugar has stabilized. So has my blood pressure. My weight is coming down. My limbs are slowly coming back. My vision and voice are returning to normal. My life seems to be coming together. I never thought I'd be so happy to reinvent myself. I truly see things in my future being much different, and I see a lot more happiness, and I am looking forward to 2024 but not to forget 2023. The year 2023 will always be the year I had my stroke of recovery!

LETTER FROM THE AUTHOR

Dear reader,

Thank you for reading my story, I hope you enjoyed it and I hope you can use my story to find strength in whatever it is you are dealing with. In my life I have found that when times seem tough, it can always get worse. Instead of inviting that into our life, consider rewriting your situation. Learn a lesson from what you're going through and be sure to process your emotions correctly. You can get through this and I believe you will. You've got this. Keep going!

www.ingramcontent.com/pod-product-compliance
Lightning Source LLC
LaVergne TN
LVHW100325210926
848480LV00003B/1263